Lost in Shadows

Susan Boyle

Copyright © 2024 by Susan Boyle

All rights reserved.

No portion of this book may be reproduced in any form without written permission from the publisher or author, except as permitted by U.S. copyright law.

Contents

1. The Crash — 1
2. The Call & Finding Out — 4
3. The Nerves — 8
4. Meeting The Brothers — 13
5. Saw That Coming — 17
6. Wasn't Supposed To Hear That — 21
7. Parking Lot Brawl — 27
8. The Mall — 33
9. The Flashback — 37
10. 1st Day of School — 41
11. First Day of School Pt. 2 — 46
12. New Friend — 52
13. Back Home — 58
14. Shaken Up — 62
15. Things Like That Don't Fly Here — 68

16. Let Them Be Scared   74

17. Is That What They Think Of Us?   79

The Crash

Tamsyn POV

It happened in the blink of an eye. One moment we were driving normally. Aspen was clutching her side where someone had stabbed her with a dagger and mom was frantically trying to stop the bleeding. Ashton was passed out. I was trying to hide the pain I was going through as I eyed the driver, ensuring he was going where he was supposed to be. And in the next second, the car was toppled over, and I lost consciousness.

....

I woke up with a dreadful pain in my head and immediately looked around for the twins. My heart dropped as I saw they were nowhere to be found, and I was lying in what looked like a hospital bed. I quickly yanked all the IVs attached to my arm off and attempted to stand up. Keyword, attempted. I tried to find my balance as my eyes got fuzzy, and I felt the dizziness start to engulf me. Right then, the doors to my room burst open and a nurse walked in.

"Miss, you can't get up ye-"

"WHERE ARE MY SIBLINGS? AND MY MOM?" I yelled, cutting her off. The nurse made me sit down and then finally started talking again.

"Your siblings are fine. Your sister has a nasty gash on her side, though." I held my breath. "I'm guessing it's a shard from a window that pierced through her skin in the crash," she concluded with a hint of pity in her voice. I let out the breath I was holding. There was no need for anyone to go digging up the real cause of that gash.

"Ashton's ok?" I asked again to reconfirm. She nodded but I could tell there was something she wasn't telling me. Then it hit me.

"Where's my mom?" Silence was all that followed. I started to get impatient. But before I could yell again, a tear escaped the nurse's eye. I couldn't do this. No. This can't be happening. Please. I was begging her with my eyes.

"I'm sorry. We did everything we could." she said simply. I was at a loss for words. I just nodded and sat back down, tears gathering in my eyes, but I didn't let them fall. Not in front of her. I asked her to take me to my siblings, and she did. When I entered the room, the silent crying assured me that I wasn't the one who would have to tell them about mom. Without a word, I went and hugged my baby siblings. We sat there for a good hour, and then the same nurse from before came in with another lady behind her. This lady was dressed in casual-formal clothing and had a few files in her arm. I separated from my siblings and stood up.

"Hello, you must be Tamsyn. I'm Maya McMiller, your social worker." the lady said, holding her hand out for a handshake. Although I hated unnecessary physical contact, especially with people I didn't know, I knew better than to anger someone who seemed to have authority. I quickly shook her hand and asked her why she was there.

"Well, Tamsyn...as you know, your mother was your only legal guardian..." I widened my eyes and remembered that although Blake was my "step-father" to the outside world, mom and him were never married....obviously. "So we did a DNA test on all three of you to check if you have any other family members that can take you in," she concluded. I heard Ashton and Aspen take a long breath as they let it all settle in. I knew we were all thinking the same thing, aren't they going to send us back to Blake...and The Guild? My thoughts were interrupted as Ms. McMiller cleared her throat to get our attention again.

"Your dad is willing to take you in." Suddenly, my legs felt weak, and I heard Ashton run to me, letting me balance my weight onto him. Although he's only thirteen and three younger than me, he's already a couple of inches taller than me.

"Are you ok, Tammie?" He asked me, his voice shaking from the revelation as well. I nodded my head and turned to Aspen, who had her hand over her mouth and her wide eyes trained straight at Ms. McMiller.

"B-but mom said he's dead..." Aspen almost whispered, her voice still weak from all the injuries she sustained. Ms.McMiller looked at her sadly and sighed. I could tell something was troubling her.

"I just got off the phone with him, and although he immediately agreed to take custody of all of you...it was almost as if he didn't know you two existed," she said, making eye contact with the twins. I could tell they were confused, and I could sense a twinge of hurt coming from Ashton's eyes.

The Call & Finding Out

Francesco's POV

My sons and I were at the dinner table. Kyler was asking Ezekiel and Everett about school. Apparently, Ezeiel finally joined a club, and I was glad he seemed to be getting better. Everett's voice was the loudest as always, and I smiled at him, silently thanking him for unknowingly keeping this household together. Sebastian was poking at his food and I saw Theodore give him a stern glance from the corner of my eyes. Sometimes, he acted more like a father than me. As I was about to say something, my phone suddenly started ringing. Everyone stopped talking and looked at me since they knew better than to be making any noise when I'm on a phone call. But I was a bit annoyed that they called in the middle of one of the only family times we get.

"Hello?" I said, uninterested.

"Hi! I'm Maya McMiller, a social worker, and I'm calling you regarding your children." the voice said as I scrunched up my eyebrows and looked at all my sons again. Theodore raised his eyebrow, wondering what this call was about.

"And why would that be? Considering I'm currently with all my children right now?" I said, my voice getting a bit deeper since the topic was now on my kids. That sentence definitely piqued some interest as Sebastian and Ezekiel lifted their heads from their phones to look at me weirdly. The rest of the conversation went by like a blur. The next thing I knew, I got up from my chair, and my hand went through my hair as I dealt with the conflicting emotions inside of me. When I got up, so did all of my sons. Theodore and Kyler looked especially concerned, and the look on their faces made it seem like they were ready to kill anyone or obey any command right now. I inwardly chuckled; this is what growing up in the mafia does to you. Before I could say anything, my youngest son spoke up.

"Dad, what's wrong?" Everett asked as he looked at his brothers, confused. I took a deep breath before deciding to tell them elsewhere, where the maids wouldn't be able to overhear.

"In my office. All of you, now," I commanded as I started walking towards the stairs, still processing all of the information. I couldn't help but smile. Tamsyn was coming home. But...how could she...how could Arella do this to me? Not letting me even know that I had two other children. Two. Whole. Children. With each thought, more anger boiled up inside of me. I sat at my desk and beckoned for my children to come in. Since Sebastian was the last, he closed the door behind him.

"We found her," I said, gazing at the confused faces forming in front of me.

"Uh...found who?" Everett asked. Before I could answer him, Theodore opened his mouth.

"Dad...her? As in..."

"T-tamsyn?" Kyler interjected hesitantly. I nodded. Kyler and Everett looked at each other and immediately had tears in their eyes and big smiles.

Theodore looked away, and I knew he felt emotional but just didn't want to show it. Sebastian was the first to say anything.

"Well, where is she? Where has she been all these years? How is she?"

"Does it even matter?! She's been gone for thirteen years. Why does she just have to appear out of nowhere now?!" Ezekiel stated harshly, earning a dark glare from all his brothers except Sebastian. He didn't really care. I knew from the start that Ezekiel wasn't going to take the information lightly, but I also knew he was going to have to work on his attitude.

"Dad, can you tell us what's going on?" Theodore asked. I slumped back onto my chair, figuring out how to word it.

"Boys, there's something else. She - Arella-" at the mention of her name, all the boys stiffened, and Ezekiel's hands started to shake, "-Arella was pregnant when she took Tamsyn," I finally said as I looked straight ahead still trying to wrap my head around it myself.

"You're joking, right?" I heard Kyler ask. I shook my head no, and I guess my solemn face confirmed it because he leaned against the wall and ran his hand through his hair with an unreadable expression. The other boys were still silent, probably fighting their own demons at the moment. Everyone loved and missed Tamsyn. She was the light of our lives. Her happy laughter and bubbly demeanor easily swayed everyone. Even if we had her only for three years, her absence struck like an earthquake. Nothing was the same ever again. Finally, I decided I needed to tell them the other part of the news.

"They're twins," I said with a firm tone. Now, all of their heads snapped up, and their mouths were gaping open. Ezekiel and Everett subconsciously looked at each other, and Everett flashed his brother a quick smile as if to reassure him. Sebastian was mumbling to himself, and Theodore looked like he wanted to kill someone.

"How dare she just hide them and never tell us?!" Theodore said, raising his voice. "It's one thing to kidnap our only little sister, but to hide frikkin twins from us?! That's another level of crazy," He finished.

"I couldn't agree more, Theo, and there isn't much time to dwell on it because Arella died, and now these kids are coming into my custody," I said. Ezekiel widened his eyes and looked like he was debating whether to say something or not. Theodore and Kyler had pained expressions on their faces that disappeared the moment they saw me glance at them. Theodore and Kyler were the only ones who really remembered their mother. It must've been hard to hear she was dead, even though they hated her after that day. "Theodore, you're coming with me, Kyler - make sure the jet is ready. Everett - get their rooms ready. Sebastian and Ezekiel....be home when we get back," I commanded them as I stood up.

The Nerves

Tamsyn's POV

I was sitting with Ashton and Aspen, impatiently waiting for our father to arrive. The nerves were unmatched. I always had a feeling that they were alive and that mom was hiding something from us, but I never tried to pry because I knew she was already going through a lot. Now, I wish I did. If he didn't know that the twins existed, it means mom left right before they were born. Ashton's hand squeezed mine, and I could feel his fingers shaking. We were scared. We were never wanted. We were never loved. The only person who tried to protect us was our mom, but even she couldn't do much. 'You three are good for nothings! You think anyone will want you now that you have so much blood on your hands?' As if reading my mind, Aspen spoke up.

"He won't even want us after he figures out what we have done," Aspen said, looking down.

"Yea, maybe we should just run away or something? Who knows, maybe he'll even send us back to...B-blake," Ashton whispered. Before I could respond to him, the door was tugged open, and two tall men walked in behind Ms. McMiller. Instinctively, all three of us stood up immediately, but I felt Aspen flinch a little when she moved so fast. That gash was bad.

"Tamsyn, Ashton, and Aspen. This is your father...and your older brother," Ms.McMiller said with a smile. Ashton and Aspen looked at each other in shock, probably upon hearing the words 'older brother' but for some reason, I wasn't overly surprised about that fact. Both the men were looking at us coldly and their auras were definitely more intimidating than Blake's. Then, the older-looking man stepped forward and introduced himself.

"Hello children, I'm Francesco Fontana, your father," he said, surprisingly softly. I was about to introduce myself but then he took his hand and lightly brushed my cheek. I flinched from the sudden contact but didn't stop him. "You must be Tamsyn...my Tammie," he said with a voice mixed with relief and sadness. He took a deep breath and looked behind me to the twins. Something in his gaze changed. It felt less warm and suddenly I was scared he wasn't going to accept them. I stepped back, trying to cover the twins from him. After he realized what I was doing, he immediately dropped his cold gaze and looked at them with hurt in his eyes.

"Ashton and Aspen...you have beautiful names," he said softly with a small smile as if to reassure them. They slowly stepped forward and responded with "Thank You" at the same time. I could tell Francesco was having a hard time figuring out what to say and that's when the other man spoke up.

"Hey. I'm Theodore, your oldest brother," he said blankly.

"Oldest brother?!" Aspen blurted out, with wide eyes. Theodore nodded.

"Yes. You have four more," he responded. Aspen looked like she was about to pass out, and Ashton stepped closer to her just in case she actually gave out. She never dealt well when it came to interacting with males, especially after what Blake would do.

Theodore's POV

Tamsyn was all grown un now. She had long curly-wavy hair and grew up to be beautiful...like mom. At first, all of my attention was on her. Analyzing her features, mannerisms, and everything about her. My father's voice brought me out of my thoughts.

"Ashton and Aspen...you have beautiful names," I heard him say, as I finally let my eyes wander to the two other figures standing slightly behind Tamsyn. The moment I laid my eyes on them, I felt the same tug at my heart that I felt for Tamsyn. My youngest siblings. Ashton looked so much like how Kyler looked when he was young and Aspen was like his female version.

When I said I was their oldest brother, Aspen's outburst surprised me. It didn't sound just shocked, but almost scared as well. I noticed how Ashton scooched closer to her and I inwardly smiled, acknowledging the act of protectiveness towards his sister.

"Let's go," I said as I walked to the door.

Third POV

Tamsyn felt an unknown sense of relief when they got on the jet. It was something about knowing she was getting further away from Blake and The Guild. Once they were strapped into their seats, Francesco started speaking again.

"So kids, since I came here on such short notice, I wasn't able to look into anything about you," he started. All three of the kids suddenly got tense as they waited for him to continue. "So what do you like, what are your hobbies?" he asked. The twins looked at Tamsyn, silently urging her to answer first.

"Um, well, I like reading and I often daydream a lot," Tamsyn said shrugging. She didn't really know what to say since they weren't allowed to have hobbies. Sometimes, their mom would sneak in a couple of books for them to read, usually educational. Since they weren't allowed to go to school, all of their education came from the books they read.

"I like playing games like charade and mafia!" Aspen said enthusiastically. Francesco and Theodore inwardly flinched at the second game but easily hid it. They were happy Aspen had finally spoken up.

"I...like drawing," Ashton said, as his eyes found the ground very interesting. He was embarrassed that it was the only thing he had done that he found fun and most people consider it a feminine hobby.

"That's great," Francesco said with a faint smile. "Why don't you three get some sleep, it's going to be a long while before we arrive," he said, "The room is to your left."

The kids looked to their left curiously, intrigued that there were beds on the jet. Ultimately though, all three of them have always had a hard time sleeping in the presence of people for the fear of waking up without each other. They were about to shake their heads no when Theodore said, "You can all go together." They looked at each other again hesitantly. It had been more than twenty-four hours since they had actually slept and it was definitely starting to get hard to keep their eyes open.

"Ok," Tamsyn said, getting up and leading her siblings to the room.

Aspen's POV

I couldn't. I couldn't do it. I could never sleep knowing those two scary-looking men were right there. I wanted to cry.

"I can't. I'll just stay up," I said weakly to my siblings. Ashton shook his head.

"No way. It's been too long since you've slept," Ashton said firmly. After he saw my defiant face he said, "Fine, I'll stay awake and watch while you sleep," he said. As good as it sounded, I knew he was sleep-deprived too and I couldn't possibly let him suffer while I got to rest peacefully.

"I'll stay awake. Both of you sleep. No questions," Tamsyn said in a firm tone. I knew better than to argue. I could tell Ashton was biting his tongue not to say anything. He hated it when Tammie protected and sacrificed her own well-being for us. But he also knew that there was no use trying to argue.

As soon as our heads hit the pillows, we were whisked away to dreamland.

Please comment if you liked the chapter and/or if you have any suggestions!

Love,

Day Lilac ♡

Meeting The Brothers

T amsyn POV

After the twins fell asleep, I walked out of the door back to where Francesco and Theodore were.

"You didn't sleep?" Francesco asked as he saw me walking out.

"No, I'm not that sleepy," I responded. And then I yawned. Crap. When did I become so careless? I mentally face-palmed myself as I smiled at them sheepishly, hoping they would forget the yawn. They obviously didn't because although they still looked emotionless, there was a hint of amusement in their eyes. I just sat back down on the seat and stared right ahead.

I didn't want to give them a chance to talk to me, so I put my head against the window and stared at the clouds as if it were the most fascinating thing ever. Thank God they got the hint and left me alone. Around three hours in, I saw Francesco get up and walk towards the room the twins were sleeping in. Without thinking, I got up and blocked the way, not letting him go in. I saw a mixture of sadness, hurt, and anger reflected in his eyes.

"Excuse me?" He asked firmly.

"You're excused," I said without thinking. The moment those words escaped my mind, I knew I messed up. I saw Theodore narrow his eyes and walk up to us.

"May I go see my children?" Francesco asked.

"No," I replied. Theodore looked at me as if I had grown two heads. Honestly, I was scared. There were two men that looked much bigger and stronger than me. If I tried, I probably would be able to hold my ground pretty well against them, but the problem is that I have nowhere to run right now. Even if I knocked them out, which I definitely could, thanks to all of The Guild's training, what would we do after? As I kept overthinking, I didn't realize Theodore was reaching his hand out to me. Instinctively, I smacked his hand away and stepped back. He looked mad.

"Listen, I wasn't going to go through the rules right now, but I think this behavior needs to be addressed," he said coldly. I tried to gulp down my fear. Rules mean punishments. "Respect. We demand respect, and in return, we'll respect you," I quickly nodded my head and tried to hide my shaking hands, still blocking the way.

"P-please don't go in...they have a hard time falling asleep and are quite sensitive to...new...noises," I mustered up, trying to make myself sound believable. Slowly, they both went and sat back down. Respect. We know how that works. But I was confused when he said he'd respect us back. It was never both ways for us. I returned to the room, sat on the floor, and waited for this flight to end.

Third POV

As the jet was getting ready for landing, the men made sure all three of them were sitting down on actual seats with their seatbelts on. Ashton and Aspen were still groggy from just waking up but were so intrigued by the landing process that they quickly got over it. Tamsyn still hadn't told them about the incident that happened when they were asleep so the twins were oblivious to the tense air between the men and their sister. Tamsyn's hands kept shaking as she was thinking whether they would be safe or be getting themselves into an even worse situation than before. 'No, nothing can be worse than The Guild and Blake....' Tamsyn kept telling herself. Ashton reached his hand out to hers and squeezed it, reassuring her that everything would be alright.

After they got out of the jet, there was a sleek black Lamborghini waiting for them. Their wide eyes didn't go unnoticed by Francesco who lightly chuckled at their reactions. They got into the car and almost immediately, Ashton and Aspen fell asleep again. Tamsyn sighed as she was left alone in her thoughts. Memories from the car crash a couple of days ago started coming back to her and she closed her eyes in an attempt to repel them from her mind.

Soon, they were in front of the house - scratch that, mansion. Remembering the fact that there would be many other men in the house, Ashton and Tamsyn subconsciously took hold of Aspen's hands.

Aspen POV

With my siblings on either side of me, I let out a breath and tried to look as confident as I could. Right as we stepped in front of the door, it swung open to reveal a guy who unmistakably resembled Ashton and me. I squeezed Ashton's hand tighter.

"Hey! I can not believe y'all are finally here!" The guy exclaimed with a big smile on his face. Behind him, another boy who looked younger came and looked just as excited.

"Alright guys, move and let us in the house," Theodore interrupted. They made way for us, and the inside of the house was even more grand than the outside, if that was even possible. I also noticed two other boys leaning against the wall. One was looking at us with no emotions, and the other had his eyes glued to his phone. He looked like he didn't want to be there at all. For some reason, I felt a little pang of sadness in my heart when I saw them.

"Ok, so we should probably introduce ourselves," the guy who looked like us said. "I'm Kyler, your second oldest brother, and I'm 24," he said.

"I'm Everett, and I'm 17! I'm so glad y'all are finally here!" another one said with a huge grin.

"Sebastian. 19," The one that was leaning on the wall said. I tried smiling at him, but he just ignored me and looked at Tamsyn a bit before looking away again. Ouch. Ashton and I did talk about how this family might not really accept us or think of us as real family in comparison to Tamsyn since they actually knew her. We two were a mistake. I saw Everett nudge the boy on his phone to introduce himself, but he didn't even glance up.

"This is Ezekiel, my amazing twin brother who can be a little grumpy at times," Everett said sheepishly. Ezekiel looked up at his phone, glared at us, and then walked off. Sebastian sighed and followed him, probably so he could get away from us.

"Ok, Everett, can you take them to their rooms?" Francesco asked, and Everett nodded while gesturing for us to follow him.

Thank you very much for reading! Please please comment if you like it and follow me as well!

Love,

Day Lilac ♡

Saw That Coming

Flashback

"Follow me!" Blake said as he yanked my hand. I tried my best to catch up to him with the terrible pain in my legs from the poison-laced bullet. He would've let me just die on other days, but he was scared I would rat them out if I were captured.

"Aspen!" Tamsyn shook me awake from that terrible flashback. I smiled at her apologetically, but not before I saw Everett's slightly confused expression.

"Sorry, I just blanked out for a second," I said to him while looking down. He smiled at me and continued walking.

"So this is Tamsyn's room, and the two across from it are Ashton's and Aspen's," he said pointing at the doors. I froze and looked at him with a slightly scared expression.

"W-wait...we can't be together?" I asked, my voice shaking.

"I mean, y'all can totally spend as much time as you want together, your rooms are just for some alone time and when you have to go to sleep," he said matter-of-factly, as if there was no other option. I have never slept away from my siblings other than...those times. I didn't even realize I was shaking until Ashton spoke up.

"Is there no way we can sleep in the same room?" he asked softly.

"You guys are not at the age to be sleeping together anymore. You will be sleeping in your separate rooms," a cold and powerful voice boomed from behind us. I twitched because it startled me and then quickly turned around to come face-to-face with Theodore and Ezekiel trailing behind him. I gulped and tugged at Tamsyn's sleeve.

"Look at her acting like a five-year-old who can't even sleep alone," Ezekiel scoffed as he rolled his eyes. Before I could say anything, he looked at Ashton.

"You too, I would've expected more from a Fontana son," he said with hatred as he walked off.

Tamsyn POV

No one talks to my little siblings like that. Before Ezekiel could walk away, I grabbed his arm and turned him around to me.

"Don't you dare talk to my siblings like that," I said in a low whisper, daring him to say something back.

"Well, what are you gonna do about it, huh?" he said smugly. Respect. It goes both ways. I kept repeating it in my head like a mantra in an attempt not to start a fight with this guy. But then he lost my respect. He shook my hand off and muttered, "unwanted b**h," under his breath.

I turned him around and did the first thing that came to my mind. I pushed him. It wasn't a hard push, but I think he was too surprised to react so he went crashing into the wall.

"Hey! So that's how you want to play this!?" He growled and got up in my face. There was nothing but anger and hatred in his voice. "How dare you talk back to me in this house which is barely even yours, because your nice little mama took you to have a better life away from us? Not to mention those other two kids. They're just strangers here. Sure, we were looking for you, Tamsyn, but those two? Those two were just a mistake." He said, venom dripping from each letter.

"EZEKIEL! GO TO YOUR ROOM NOW!" Francesco's voice boomed from behind us.

Aspen POV

Those two were just a mistake. A mistake. Mistake. Ezekiel was right. We were a mistake. Mom didn't even know she was pregnant with us until after she left. She must've been heartbroken about it too. Imagine having two more children with the man she just left. I hated this feeling. After Francesco told Ezekiel to go to his room, all three of us shut ourselves in Tamsyn's room, not wanting to face everyone else.

"You're not weak; you know that, right?" Tamsyn said, looking at Ashton. He gave her a lopsided grin. A grin only we have ever seen because he's never himself in front of anyone else. Seeing him smile, made me smile, which made Tamsyn smile, and I could just feel the presence of mom smiling too.

"Yea duh, they don't call me the little devil for no reason," he said, rolling his eyes. I started feeling better, but I still couldn't settle the terrible feeling I had in the pit of my stomach. And that nasty gash wasn't helping one bit. I bit my tongue so that I didn't make a noise when I ran my hand over it.

Third POV

"Ezekiel, what the hell was that!?" Francesco yelled at the boy. The rest of the brothers were also gathered in their dad's office with knowing looks.

"What do you mean? You know very well we were doing just fine without them," Ezekiel practically hissed.

"You know I'm not going to tolerate this behavior," Francesco said through gritted teeth. Ezekiel rolled his eyes before responding.

"C'mon, don't act like you suddenly love those strangers."

"They are my children."

"Yeah, pathetic excuses for your children. Do you not realize how weak they are?"

"Give. Me. Your. Phone. You're grounded for a week."

Ezekiel scoffed and gave his phone to his dad. He saw it coming.

"You should be lucky you're getting off so easy," Theodore told his younger brother.

Hope you guys liked this chapter!

Love,

Day Lilac ♡

Wasn't Supposed To Hear That

Tamsyn POV

I woke up with a throbbing headache and a grumbling stomach. I looked at the digital clock at the bedside, which read 02:23 AM. I got up from the bed and saw my two siblings cuddling close together at the other end of the bed. After coming to my room following the interaction with Ezekiel, we didn't feel like leaving the room and then we ended up falling asleep before dinner. But they probably wouldn't have called us for dinner anyway...

The headache wouldn't go away, and I couldn't fall asleep, so I decided to go look for something to ease the pain in my head or at least something to put in my stomach. Hopefully, no one will be awake at the time. I threw on one of the hoodies Ashton brought along and quietly creaked the door open. Thank goodness for my photographic memory, because without it, I would have been lost in a matter of seconds. Once I found what was probably the kitchen, I started hearing hushed voices.

"Are you happy we found them?" a voice I recognized as Kyler said.

"Of course I am...they're just different," Theodore said. "As Fontanas, I don't know how to deal with them," he said as he sighed. I tensed as I realized that they thought that we weren't worthy of being a part of their family.

"Ashton and Aspen...even saying their names feels so foreign," a new voice, probably Sebastian, said. I decided against entering the kitchen, so I turned to leave. The moment I turned my head, my body went stiff, and my eyes went wide. It was Everett. How long was he here? How did I not detect him? Is he going to punish me for eavesdropping?

But instead of seeing anger in his eyes, I saw hurt and a sense of apology. But that anger didn't seem directed at me, instead, he seemed angry at his brothers. Before he was able to make our presence known to the boys on the other side of the wall, I shook my head signaling for him to just forget about it. 'Please don't tell them I overheard them,' I practically begged with my eyes. Somehow, he understood and nodded before holding his hand out to me. Hesitantly, I reached out to it and wrapped my fingers around his warm hand. He smiled faintly at me and led me back to my room.

When we got to my door, he let go of my hand and took a deep breath.

"I'm so sorry. They shouldn't have been saying those things. I swear they love you and the twins. They're just not used to it yet," he whispered. His face showed nothing but sincerity. I immediately knew that Everett was the only one who felt like my brother, other than Ashton of course. I think being only one year apart helps with that connection. Although, technically Ezekiel is also only one year older than me....but he's just different I guess.

Everett gently poked my forehead to shake me out of my thoughts.

"Thank you," I whispered to him and opened the door to my room, only to be met with Ashton's scared eyes as he whisper yelled at me.

"Where were you?! When I woke up, you were just gone!?" He seemed like he was about to say something else as well but then suddenly stopped when he saw Everett.

"Hey, why are you even awake lil bro?" he said to Ashton, who was still recovering from seeing Everett with me.

"Did he do anything to you? Why do you look so sad, Tammie?" Ashton asked me, worry laced in his words.

"Why would I do anything to her?" Everett asked, confusion evident in his face.

"No, Ashton, I'm fine. He was just showing me the way back after I went to the kitchen for some water," I replied, cutting them both off. Ashton hesitantly nodded and made way for me to come inside. I bid goodnight to Everett and closed the door.

Ashton POV

Lil bro. He just called me his little brother. I couldn't help but let myself feel a little warm on the inside.

Tamsyn POV

After much effort, I was finally able to get some sleep, but I was still bombarded with tiring nightmares. But I was thankful that it wasn't as bad as usual.

I woke up at 7 AM and decided to get ready for the day. I hopped into the shower because no one told us we couldn't, and I would take advantage of it. After a ten-minute, cold shower, I got out and put Ashton's hoodie back on. I brushed my hair and put it in a high ponytail with some pieces framing my face. I left the bathroom to see the twins groggily getting up and stretching. Once they saw me get out, they both looked at each other and sprinted to the bathroom, hoping to take a shower first. I rolled my eyes as I heard them start arguing about who can go in first. Finally, Aspen ended up winning after a heated tournament of rock-paper-scissors. Ashton came and sat next to me on the bed as we waited for her to finish. After around five minutes, which was quite short for Aspen, the water stopped and I heard her voice through the door.

"Tammie? Can you come here for a sec?" I quickly got up and made my way to the bathroom. I slowly creaked open the door and was met with Aspen wrapped in a towel. But she looked like she was in pain and there was blood dripping on the floor.

"Aspen! What happened?" I asked, rushing towards her. I turned around to close the door behind me and saw Ashton up from the bed with a worried look on his face.

"Is everything okay?" He asked.

"Yeah...just...it's okay."

I told Aspen to sit down on the toilet seat cover as I slowly removed her towel, revealing the gash that I thought healed.

"Aspen! I thought this was healed!" I gently 'yelled' at her while rummaging through the cabinets, trying to find something to bandage it with.

"I-it was, but then it started opening again," Aspen said, pain evident in her voice.

"Aspen, this looks really bad. I think we might have to te-"

"No! You can't tell them! They're going to think I'm even more weak," Aspen said defeatedly. "Please, Tammie..."

I sighed and then asked Ashton to give me one of the pillowcases from the bed. It was small but big enough to tie around Aspen's slim waist.

"If it gets infected, you tell me immediately," I told her in my most commanding voice. She nodded quickly, put her clothes on, and left the bathroom, only to be met with the overprotective sibling #2.

"What happened? Is that blood? Don't tell me it's from that stab?" Ashton interrogated the moment she went out.

"Don't worry, it's patched up now," Aspen responded. As Ashton was about to refute, I told him to hurry up and shower so that we could go downstairs together.

He reluctantly obliged, and then I went to my torn backpack to fetch a small orange container. There was one painkiller left.

"I don't need it," Aspen immediately said as she saw me holding it.

"Yes, you do, Aspen. You're either going to take this or pass out in front of everyone and leave me having to explain," I deadpanned. That seemed to convince her as she grabbed the pill from my hand and swallowed it dry. After a couple of minutes, Ashton came out, and we all went downstairs together. It seemed like chaos. Sebastian, Ezekiel, and Everett were running around, seemingly trying to find something, while Kyle was attempting and, without a doubt, failing at trying to make food. Theodore and Francesco weren't there.

"Um...hi," I said, making our presence known. The boys stopped scavenging around for a millisecond; Everett gave us a big smile, the other two ignored us, and then they went on with what they were doing.

"Hey, kids. Don't mind all this. The boys need to go to school in like," Kyle looked at his watch, "well...five minutes ago, so I'm just quickly making them breakfast," he said. I nodded and sat down on a chair at the table, the twins beside me.

"Something smells burnt," Aspen muttered while sniffing the air. I peeked over Kyle's shoulder to be met with the scene of eggs that looked almost inedible. I scrunched my nose as I sighed.

"Let me do it," I said as I gently moved Kyle out of the way. Before he could protest, I took the spoon from his hand and scooped the burnt eggs off of the pan.

I quickly cracked a couple of eggs, put them in the pan, and made scrambled eggs. I added butter and cheese and asked Kyle for bread. I buttered them and put them in a different pan to heat up. Then, I quickly made sandwiches for the boys and put them on the table.

Hope you guys liked this chapter!

Love,

Day Lilac ♡

Parking Lot Brawl

Third POV

With Sebastian, Ezekiel, and Everett at school and Francesco and Theodore at work, the house was relatively peaceful. Kyler stayed home so the kids weren't home alone and did his work from his office.

"Hey guys! Are y'all hungry?" Kyler asked as he knocked on the kids' door. Tamsyn opened the door.

"I mean...we did have breakfast, so we're not really hungry," she answered.

"Nonsense, that was more than five hours ago. You must be hungry," he said. Tamsyn and the twins looked at each other and shook their heads. The breakfast they had would be enough for another a couple of days as well. Hesitantly, Kyler finally gave in and let them be without eating lunch for the time being.

Tamsyn POV

After we finally got Kyler to leave us alone to eat lunch, I turned my head to the pile of books that he gave us so that we wouldn't be bored. I looked at the book at the top of the pile and it said, Percy Jackson. I've never heard of that book before. The only books we've ever read were educational or bibliographies. Aspen peered over at the book, Percy Jackson and picked it up curiously. After skimming through the back and first few pages, she sat on the bed and started reading it. Ashton was sitting on the bed as well, leaning against her, and soon fell asleep.

It was 3.15 PM, and the boys were supposed to come back from school soon, so I decided to take a quick nap as well before chaos ensued.

Everett POV

Ezekiel and I were waiting at the school parking lot for Sebastian to drive us home. I was leaning against the car, and I still couldn't shake the weird feeling from my heart.

"Hey, why are being such a jerk today, huh?" Ezekiel snapped at me. This entire day has just been terrible because all I have been thinking about was my brothers talking shit about my younger siblings...and even though Ezekiel wasn't a part of that conversation, he was still treating them like shit.

"Me?! A jerk? Have you been hearing yourself these days?" I snapped back at him. His eyes darkened, and I could tell something in him tore.

"Don't tell me you're defending those stupid kids," he said angrily.

"Don't call them stupid kids. Those kids are your younger siblings!" I yelled back.

"I. Don't. Care. I have nothing to do with them," he said through gritted teeth. I couldn't do it anymore. I stepped closer to him and swiftly pushed him. Watching him stumble backward put a smirk on my face. Obviously, he wouldn't just take it. So I dodged a punch to my face and tackled him to the ground. Ezekiel is stronger than me in most ways and actual fights, but this wasn't a fight with an enemy, it was more of a 'cooling off' fight.

But it got quite heated; at one point, there was blood on both of our faces. As I was about to deliver a punch to my dear brother's face, I felt a pair of strong hands break us apart.

"What the hell, guys?" Sebastian asked, looking confused. Ezekiel and I aren't known to get into fights, and the last time we did, we both cried while apologizing to each other because we couldn't stand seeing each other hurt. I was broken out of my thoughts as I felt Sebastian wiping the blood from my face worriedly. He then turned to Ezekiel and grabbed his bruised hands, wiping the blood from them as well.

"Do y'all wanna talk about it?" Sebastian asked the both of us.

"No," we both said at the same time, and then glared at each other. Sebastian just sighed and unlocked the car door, then sat in the driver's seat. I sat in the passenger seat, and Ezekiel was in the back. Sebastian looked at us one last time, trying to hide the worry in his eyes. He was the biggest aloof and 'I don't care about anything' sibling out of all of us, so seeing him worry about us actually made me feel a little bad. It was silent the whole ride back.

When we entered the house, I was expecting it to be a little more noisy than usual, considering there were three more people living here now, but it was as silent as it could be.

"Kiiids~~~ welcome home!" Kyler's voice resonated through the hallway.

"Ky, can you get the first aid kit?" Sebastian asked out to him.

"What, wh-" he started, but then stopped midsentence when he saw Ezekiel and I.

"What happened!? Did someone attack you guys?!" he said frantically as he came up to us to look at our wounds more closely. Ezekiel just grunted and attempted to walk upstairs to his room but was grabbed by Kyler, who looked at him sternly.

"Not so soon, we're gonna patch y'all up, and then you're going to explain what the hell happened," he said firmly. This time, it was Sebastian who attempted to walk away.

"You too, Seb," Kyler said.

"But I didn't even do anything," Sebastian grumbled as he took a seat on the couch.

Ezekiel stayed quiet in the 'explaining ourselves' segment of the interaction as I went off about how he deserved way worse.

"So you guys fought each other?" Kyler asked said, raising an eyebrow. We nodded. He sighed and started treating our wounds without another word.

"Just letting you know, I'm gonna have to tell Dad about this," he said.

"Yea, whatever, but where's Tamsyn and the twins?" I asked, suddenly remembering how quiet it was in the house.

"Um, they've just been in their room the whole day," Kyler shrugged.

"Useless," Ezekiel muttered under his breath, and Sebastian just rolled his eyes.

~timeskip~

Third POV

The entire family was gathered in the living room since Francesco called for a family meeting that night.

"Alright, since you guys didn't bring many things with you, y'all are going to go shopping tomorrow for everything you need," Francesco said to the twins and Tamsyn.

"It's okay, we really don't need anything," Tamsyn answered while playing with her fingers nervously.

"No, it's not okay; you three will be going to the mall tomorrow with Everett, Ezekiel, and Theodore. Kyler and Sebastian have some work to do with me, so they won't be able to tag along," he said.

"Why do I have to go?" Ezekiel asked angrily but shut up when he saw his dad's expression.

"Make sure you get supplies for school," Francesco said lastly as Aspen, Ashton, and Tamsyn's faces all dropped with eyes wide.

"S-school?" Aspen asked quietly.

"Mhmm, you'll be starting on Monday with Everett and Ezekiel. Technically, Sebastian already graduated, but he's interning as a teacher assistant there right now, so he'll be there as well," he said. He paused as he looked at the kids's scared expressions and asked, "You guys have been going to school, right?" he asked. The kids looked at each other uneasily, and then finally Tamsyn spoke up.

"Um, we've never been to an actual school before; we were homeschooled our entire lives," she said, trying to make sure her voice wasn't shaking.

"Homeschooled? I remember...your mom...hated the idea of homeschooling kids. Something about learning how to live in the real world or something?" Theodore said, confused. Francesco was also a little confused since he knew how much their mother was against the idea of homeschooling.

"She liked teaching us herself," Aspen said, shrugging. Although still doubtful, they just left it be thinking that Arella (their mom) must have changed a lot after leaving.

I really hope you guys liked this chapter! Please vote and follow!

Love,

Day Lilac ♡

The Mall

~ At the mall~

Tamsyn POV

I've been to the mall once because of a kill mission on someone acting as a Starbucks barista. To say the least, these types of places have always overwhelmed me. The twins, on the other hand, were fascinated. Kyler noticed their awed expressions and chuckled.

"Y'all are acting like this is your first time in a mall," he said. Ashton and Aspen quickly looked away while trying to hide their faces. Kyler's eyes widened as he quickly looked at me to confirm his suspicions.

"Wait...have you guys actually never been to a mall before?" Everett asks slowly after seeing our reactions. I grimace as I realize I can't lie about this.

"Uuuh...our mom wasn't a fan," I said, trying to shrug it off. At this, even Ezekiel furrowed his eyebrows and shared a knowing glance at Kyler. I didn't know what it meant, but hopefully, it wasn't a big deal.

We went to a bunch of stores, and despite our constant refusal, they kept putting more stuff in the cart for each of us. After a couple of hours, the boys seemed hungry, so we went to the food court. We ordered Taco Bell, and honestly, I quite enjoyed it.

I felt a tap on my shoulder and I turned around to see Aspen.

"I need to use the restroom," she said quietly. I looked around and saw the restroom signs a little farther away from where we were.

"Ok, I'll come with you," I said as I got up to walk with her. I could tell Ashton was torn about whether to come with us or not. Out of habit, he would have come with us and waited outside, but the other brothers would have sensed something weird about that. I gave him a look to tell him to just stay while we went. He nodded and continued eating.

Ashton POV

Once my sisters left, I suddenly felt vulnerable to all the other men on the table. It was the first time I was alone with the other boys, and I already didn't like it. I tried to consume the taco I was eating as if it were the most interesting thing I had ever seen in my life. Much to the contrary of what I wanted, Kyler cleared his throat and started talking.

"So Ashton. You aren't much of a talker, are you?" he asked, breaking the silence. I just nodded and hummed a yes.

"C'mon kid, don't think you're too good to respond to him verbally," Ezekiel scoffed. I tensed my shoulders and looked down.

"Oh my god bro, cut it out," Everett scolded his twin.

"Yea, he's probably too sensitive to deal with us since he's just grown up around sisters his entire life," Ezekiel argued back. I hated the way he said sisters, as if the word held poison in it. I looked up and glared at him, my eyes finally registering the cold look in his.

"Oh, look at that, the little chick is angry," he said amusingly. I knew better than to let it get to me, but I was suddenly brought back to when Blake would play manipulation games with me to get me to torture his prisoners by telling me that I was weak and useless. Before I knew it, I was shaking, and I felt heat rising in my chest. No! I can't have a panic attack right now. I can't!

I felt a warm hand take mine, and my eyes fell on Everett's soft eyes.

"Hey, you ok lil bro?" I stared at him for a couple of seconds before feeling the heat subside, and my body felt stable again.

"Y-yea sorry, I think I had a brain freeze," I said, cringing at my own excuse as I eyed the baja blast that I barely even touched. He raised his eyebrow but didn't argue. I looked up to see Kyler looking as if he was in deep thought. I tried my best to ignore them and mentally willed my sisters to hurry up.

As if my twin telepathy worked, I see Aspen walking towards us with Tamsyn trailing behind her. I instantly perked up and shot them a quick smile. Aspen smiled back and ruffled my hair before sitting down.

"Hey! My hair was actually looking good today!" Aspen just smirked and rolled her eyes.

~Timeskip~ ~Back at the house~

Kyler POV

After the kids got their things sanctioned and in their rooms, I went to Theo's office, where I saw him and dad conversing about a recent shipment. They looked at me when I entered and immediatcly hardened their faces when they saw that I looked serious. I closed the door behind me and ran my hands through my hair before taking a seat on one of the chairs.

"Did something happen?" dad asked me curiously. Theo took a seat closer to me, and dad leaned against the desk.

"It's about the kids," I sighed. Both of them immediately looked concerned.

"Which ones? Everyone in this house except us are kids," dad asked with a 'duh' attitude in his voice.

"Tamsyn, Ashton, and Aspen." they were silent, waiting for me to continue. "Don't you guys feel like something is off?" I asked.

"I think it's just because of the sudden change...and they did just lose their mother. Maybe we're being too insensitive to that fact," dad said.

"But don't think it's weird that they were homeschooled, never ate McDonald's before, and even never went to a mall before?" I asked again. They looked surprised at the last revelation because we all knew how much our mom loved malls.

"She probably just changed," Theodore said harshly before turning around to look out the window. Dad seemed to agree, so I decided to leave it be.

Thank you guys for reading this chapter! Please let me know what y'all think. Please vote and follow!

Love,

Day Lilac ♡

The Flashback

Third POV

"Hey, dad and Theodore want you guys in Theo's office right now," Everett said after entering Tamsyn's room.

~flashack~

Tamsyn POV

"In my office. Now," Blake said sternly. Aspen and I limped our way to the 'office' and awaited our punishment. Our last mission wasn't a failure. We never fail. But one of Blake's ace men was captured and it was because of us. His name was Cam, and honestly, I was a bit disappointed in myself too. We were in the middle of ruining a drug and weapon deal between two of the biggest mafias in the world. Although we succeeded, we ended up being caught while we were trying to flee the scene. The gun was aimed at me, but Cam pushed me out of the way and in return was nicked by the bullet himself. I tried to help him, but he ordered me to run and not look back. I don't know why he did it.

"Take off your clothes," I heard him say. I widened my eyes as I realized he was talking to Aspen.

"NO! I'll do it! Please, it was my fault!" I begged as I ran to Aspen. He grabbed a fist full of my hair and aggressively pushed me to the floor.

"As if, that would be letting you off easy, sweetie-pie," he said, grinning. "Alright, Aspen. Take them off. Right. Now," he said, emphasizing every word. I got up again and put my hands in front of her, trying to cover her from his view. He just smirked and punched me in the stomach. When I got up again, he punched me again.

"Tammie, no, i-it's ok," I heard Aspen's weak voice say from behind. "Please, I don't want you to get hurt," her voice broke me. Suddenly, Blake grabbed my shirt and ripped it off me. At this, Aspen ran to me and grabbed my hands in fear. Blake looked down at us and pulled me up and away from her grasp. He trailed his fingers from my waist up to my chest and then took a knife out of his pocket. Without wasting a second, he turned me so my back faced him and started cutting my back. It was in no specific order of pattern, but it hurt the same. I toned out Aspen's screams as I tried my best not to fall unconscious. At one point, I was thrown to the floor, while my blood was pooling around me. As my vision started to blur, I saw Blake pulling Aspen up from the ground and putting his gross hands all over her body. I willed myself to stay awake, but my body failed me, and I slipped out of consciousness.

Ashton's POV from that time

When I woke up, Aspen and Tamsyn were both nowhere to be seen. Worriedly, I looked around to find mom slumped against the wall in our 'room,' which was actually the basement, her lifeless eyes staring at the wall.

"Mama, where's Aspen and Tammie?" I asked her as gently as I could. She looked at me with eyes full of pain and regret.

"With Blake,"

I didn't waste a second to zoom to the 'office' cursing under my breath. When I got there, the door was shut and locked. When I got closer, my heart sank as I heard Aspen's voice.

"Please, please, please don't do it. I beg you, please," her shaky voice begged.

"Funny you think I'll listen to you, little whore. You should be happy that one even wants to look at you with your ugly face and scar-stricken body. You should be happy at least I can enjoy this body of yours," Blake said. I couldn't take it anymore. My sister.

"NO!" I yelled as I banged on the door. "LET HER GO YOU MONSTER!" I just heard a low chuckle from the other side and Aspen's little voice calling out to me.

"Let's start, shall we?" I hear Blake say. The blood in my body runs cold as I try slamming my body into the door, trying to make it budge. I banged on the door, kicked the door, and body-slammed it. Either it was made of iron, or I was just that weak. With every scream, sob, and whimper from Aspen, I kicked the door harder and harder with tears gathering in my eyes. Finally, after what felt like hours, Blake opened the door and looked at me with a smirk. His pants were undone and he was putting his shirt back on. I didn't feel like myself. I lunged at him. To say he was surprised was an understatement. I never went against him. I barely even talked back to him. But this was too much. This was my sister, who was still a baby. I knew I was a better fighter than him, and he knew it too, but what stopped me was Aspen's weak whimpers, and I suddenly remembered I had more important things to do. I pushed Blake away and went into the office, shutting the door behind me. I rushed to Aspen and wrapped my arms around her body. Her sobs slowly got louder, and she clung on to me as if her life depended on it. It killed me to see her like this. I scanned the room, and my eyes fell on Tamsyn's limp body with a pool of blood surrounding her in the corner of the room. I quickly covered Aspen with my jacket and laid her against the wall so that I could go see Tamsyn.

I was almost scared to check her pulse. Thankfully, her heart was still beating strong, but she lost way too much blood. I quickly applied pressure on her wounds and wrapped it with a piece of cloth. She groaned and tried opening her eyes, but I swiftly closed her eyes again.

"No, it's okay. You need to rest," I murmured to her, partially just not wanting her to see Aspen.

"B-but A-aspen," she barely croaked out. I shushed her, telling her that everything is okay.

Everything was not ok.

What do y'all think so far? Please vote and follow!

Love,

Day Lilac ♡

1st Day of School

Third POV

Thankfully, Everett left the room right after delivering the message, so he didn't see the breakdown all three of them almost had. 'The office' never meant anything good.

Tamsyn POV

We knocked on the door and went in when we heard a "come in!" from the inside. It had a very simplistic and modern look, much different than 'the office' we were used to.

"Why do you guys look like you've seen a ghost? You're not in trouble," Theodore said as he observed us. We quickly regained our composure and listened to what they had to say.

"Okay, there are a couple of rules you three have, especially since you'll be starting school on Monday. First rule is respect. You will respect us, and we will respect you. Second rule, no lies. We accept the truth and the truth only. Third rule, no dating. You may have friends of the opposite gender, but I expect there to be firm boundaries. Fourth rule, you're not to ever go in the basement," Theodore finished. I shuddered at the mention of the basement. I'm glad we're not allowed to go there, it means we'll never be taken there.

After being told the rules, Theodore told Everett to help us figure out what we needed to for school and get everything ready. It was only Saturday, but I knew that all three of us would be too anxious to be doing anything productive tomorrow.

Everett told us all we needed was a notebook and pencil. Ashton took that to heart and packed just that. Aspen and I explored the world of pencil pouches. I was specifically fascinated by all the different types of highlighters, pens, and pencils we can put in it.

~timeskip - morning of the first day of school~

Tamsyn POV

Somehow, the first day of school got me more nervous than I would be when I was on a mission to end someone's life. I woke up an hour before I had to and just stared at the ceiling before my alarm started ringing. I quickly shook my siblings awake, and we started getting ready. When we went downstairs, there were pancakes and mango juice ready for all three of us, and I looked around to see Ezekiel and Everett on the couch, looking like they were about to go back to sleep.

"Um, aren't you guys going to eat?" I asked quietly.

"Nah, we're used to not eating breakfast at home," Everett said as he yawned.

"So who made this?" I asked again.

"Seb did, and then he went to finish getting ready," he said. I smiled to myself and started eating.

The car ride to school was quiet, but I could almost hear my nerves churning inside of me. Aspen and Ashton were starting as freshmen, and I was starting as a junior, while the twins were seniors. I was a little sad about the fact that I wouldn't have anyone I know with me, and I felt even worse when I learned that there was Lunch A and B. Aspen and Ashton, along with Ezekiel, had Lunch A, while I had Lunch B with Everett. I was secretly glad I at least had Everett, but I knew that he had his own friends, and we probably wouldn't even cross paths.

After we parked and got out of the car, Everett and Ezekiel were immediately swarmed with a bunch of other kids that seemed like what people would call 'jocks.' Sebastian was followed by two beautiful girls with long blonde hair and clothes that were barely covering anything. He didn't seem to mind and even smiled at them.

Ashton, Aspen, and I went to the main office together to get our schedules. I looked at the lady at the desk and smiled at her, trying to get on her good side.

"Hi, we're new and here to get our schedules?" I said, sounding more like a question at the end.

"Ok! Can I have your last names?" She asked warmly.

"Uh, Fontana," I bit my tongue before I said 'I think". I still wasn't used to that last name, partially because I don't feel like a Fontana per se. The lady's eyes widened at my words and nodded immediately as she searched for our papers. She quickly handed them to us and subtly shooed us away as if she couldn't bear to have us in her office any longer.

"Look! Ashton and I have all of our classes together except Math!" Aspen said as we were walking to our first-period class. I smiled at them warmly, ignoring the sadness in my heart that I would be separated from them for the entire day. I walked them to their class and squeezed their hands before making the way to mine.

I got to my class early and picked the table at the very end, where no one was sitting yet. My head snapped to the door when I heard loud voices laughing. Two tall boys, probably as tall as Everett and Ezekiel, walked in as all the girls' attention focused on them. They lazily pulled out the chairs of the table in front of mine and sat on the side where their backs were facing me. I sighed in relief for the fact that I wouldn't have to face them every day. Don't get me wrong, they were insanely good-looking and all, but from the looks of the other girls, I don't know if I wanted to involve myself in that mess. As I was racking my brain about that situation, I almost didn't notice another boy and two girls walking up to my table.

"Hey, mind if we sit here?" the boy asked but didn't wait for me to answer as he pulled out the chair in front of me, effectively blocking my view of the two pretty boys.

"Hey! That was rude!" One of the girls said as she slapped the boy on the arm. He just rolled his eyes and focused his attention on his phone. The girl rolled her eyes, mesmerizing eyes, might I add, and smiled at me apologetically.

"So is it ok?" the other girl standing next to her asked.

"Oh y-yea, sorry I blanked for a second," I quickly said, moving a little so that they had more space to occupy the table. They both smiled at me and murmured small thank yous.

"So my name is Alina!" the girl with the pretty eyes said. They were a shade of green and especially popped because of her tan skin. She had long, wavy brown hair that was braided in a French braid.

"I'm Rosie," the other girl who had her black hair in a wolf-cut said.

"I'm Tamsyn," I said softly. I looked in front of me and was met with the boy's piercing blue eyes.

"Are you new?" He asked. I nodded and looked back at the girls. They looked at me with curious glances. Oh shit. I forgot to come up with a backstory. I bit my lips before smiling again. It's okay, lying is my forte.

"I just moved here," I said softly and let my eyes look down while I purposefully tensed my shoulders to give off the impression that it's not something I want to talk about. I just wasn't in the mood to explain anything, and I'm sure the twins wouldn't want anyone to know they have such a pathetic sister like me.

They got the 'hint', and our teacher soon distracted us.

What do y'all think so far? It would mean a lot to me if y'all voted!!

Love,

Day Lilac ♡

First Day of School Pt. 2

Tamsyn POV

"You good?" Alina asked as she waved her hand in front of my face.

"Yeah, sorry, just zoned out for a sec," I said, rubbing my eyes in an attempt to stay awake.

"Yeah, I could tell," the boy in front of me scoffed, his eyes still glued to his phone.

"Do you have a problem with me?" I finally snapped. The entire class period, he's been ignoring me like I didn't exist and has been only opening his mouth to make snarky comments. He looked up at me as if he were surprised I even spoke up and narrowed his eyes at me.

"What? No," he said, although his tone said otherwise.

"Tamsyn, don't mind him. He's always like that to new people," Alina chirped up from beside me.

"Well, he'll need to fix his attitude because I don't tolerate blatant disrespect like that," I said while raising my voice just a notch. The boy put his phone down and glared at me before turning his body to face Rosie who was sitting beside him.

"Do you hear a mouse or something?" He asked her just loud enough for me to hear. Rosie widened her eyes and slapped him lightly on his head. Well, if there's something I learned today, it's that this boy gets slapped quite frequently.

I decided against replying to his remarks and turned my attention to Alina, who had been trying to get my attention for the past couple of minutes.

"So can I call you Tammie?" she asked, hope shining through her eyes. I widened my eyes at her and immediately nodded my head. The only people who have ever called 'Tammie' were Asher, Aspen, and my mom. Hearing Alina call me by my nickname made me feel all fuzzy and cozy inside, and I couldn't help but feel happy. She suddenly grinned at me amusingly, and I looked at her a little confused.

"Wow, I didn't know you could even smile that big," Alina said while chuckling. I felt heat rise to my cheeks as I quickly turned around. After class was over, Rosie and Alina stood at both of my sides and insisted on walking me to my next class. I gladly obliged since I didn't even know where it was anyway. Without our teacher breathing down our necks, we were able to talk more freely in the hallway. I slowly felt myself letting loose and allowing my sarcastic and goofy side to peek through.

Once we got to my second-period class, I bid them goodbye and realized that the boy was trailing behind us the entire time. I looked at the three of them, this time the boy in the middle, as they walked away. Remind me to ask for his name next time I see him.

Second period went by in a blur and honestly, I missed having Rosie and Alina next to me.

In third period, we had assigned seats, and low and behold, guess who was on my table?

The first two boys who came to the table were the good-looking guys from first period. I made sure to avert my eyes from them and not gawk and to be completely honest, they weren't really my type. I just wanted to make sure the other girls in the class knew that too. The seat right in front of me was empty, but then, halfway into the class, the boy walked in with his head in his phone and stopped right in front of me. He looked up from his phone, and I swore I heard a sigh escape his lips when his eyes settled on me. I couldn't help myself; I sighed, too. He quickly dabbed up the two other boys at the table and sat down. A couple of minutes later, our teacher gave us some free time till the end of class. As I was about to lay my head on the desk for a couple of minutes of bliss, one of the guys sitting beside me poked my shoulder with his pencil.

"Oye!" I whisper-yelled, glaring at him. He had sandy blonde hair and blue eyes, and the attention he was giving me was already earning me looks from the other girls.

"Dang, you're a feisty one, aren't you," he said, smirking. I ignored him and focused my attention back on my desk. And then I felt a poke again. And again, after I didn't react.

"Bro, just leave her alone," the other guy with brown hair and light brown eyes said. I thanked him in my brain because after that, his friend finally stopped poking me.

I looked over to the name tags on the sides of the table and saw that the blondie's name was Gale, and the brown-haired one was Eren. I looked over to the boy's side of the table, but I just saw that his nametag had been ripped off. I decided it wasn't that big of a deal and put my head on the table, successfully this time.

I felt a light tap on my shoulder and slowly opened my eyes. Damn. There is no way I actually fell asleep. I quickly lifted my head from the table and was blinded by the bright lights of the classroom. And the classroom was empty. I tilted my head to see the person who had woken me up and was surprised to see the boy standing next to me, his jet-black hair covering his hazel eyes, so I couldn't tell what he was thinking.

"Good Morning, sleepyhead," he said smugly. I rubbed my eyes and looked at him in confusion.

"Why are you still here?" I responded.

"I just wanted to see your face when you realized that you just missed half of lunch," he said. My eyes widened, and I slapped my head for being so stupid. My goal was to just go to lunch and sit somewhere first so that I wouldn't have to ask anyone if I could sit with them. I groaned and was about just to put my head back on the table when I felt the boy lightly tug my hand.

"What!?" I snapped, glaring at him.

"Calm down; this teacher hates it when her students stay in class after she leaves without permission. You should probably leave," he said while putting his hands up in surrender. I hesitated before finally getting up and swinging my backpack over my shoulder. When the boy didn't make a move to walk outside with me, I stopped and looked at him in confusion.

"Wha- oh right. Do you know the way to the cafeteria?" he asked. I looked down and slightly shook my head. I heard him sigh and walk out of the door. I took that as a sign to follow him and did just that.

Soon, we were in the cafeteria, and my eyes immediately found Everett on a table surrounded by a bunch of people, most of them looked like what you would call 'jocks'. He had two girls basically on his lap, whispering things in his ear. I averted my eyes from the scene before he realized I was staring and let myself be covered by the boy's body. I didn't realize I just kept following him until we got to a table, and I snapped my head up at the sound of a familiar voice.

"Tammie!" I heard Alina exclaim. I smiled weakly at her as I scanned the table she was at. It was just her, Rosie, and now the boy also joined them. I was about to turn around when I felt a tug at my hand again. I fought myself not to flinch at the physical contact and glanced back to see Alina looking at me curiously.

"Where are you going?" she asked.

"Uuh, to find a place to sit?" I replied, looking a little unsure. At my words, the boy stifled a laugh and gazed at me in a scrutinizing manner.

"As if you have any friends. You're just gonna look like a loner," he scoffed. I pursed my lips and was about to take my leave when I realized my hand was still in Alina's grasp, and she didn't let go.

"Nuh-uh. You're sitting with us," she said to me, determined.

"Bu-

"No buts, come on," Rosie said, making space for me beside her. What was I gonna do, reject the offer? The boy was technically correct; if I left, I would just look like a loner.

I shyly let Alina tug me to the table and sat down next to Rosie. There wasn't much time left for lunch, so I didn't even bother taking out my food to eat. Instead, I got to know Alina and Rosie a bit more. Turns out it is 'absolutely despicable' that I have never seen 'The Summer I Turned Pretty' or 'The Hunger Games' ever in my life.

What do y'all think so far? Please, please, please vote and follow!

Love,

Day Lilac ♡

New Friend

A spen POV

"You two are the new kids, huh," the old lady said as she came up to our table.

"Yes, ma'am," Ashton and I said at the same time. She narrowed her eyes at us and slapped two packets of papers on my table, signaling that one of them was for Ashton. I nodded my head as I handed him a packet and muttered a thank you.

"I have a feeling she doesn't really like us," Ashton whispered to me. I smiled in agreement but was really a little disheartened. I can't believe it's only the first period, and we already got someone to hate us.

"Don't worry about it, she hates everyone," a voice from behind startled me. I turned my head to be met with a guy with a huge smile and fluffy brown hair enveloping his features.

"You sure about that? She seemed to really despise our guts the moment we walked in," Ashton responded.

"Nah, you're good. She's just worse with y'all cuz you're new," the other guy responded. Ashton nodded his head and then seemed to remember something.

"Oh, I'm Ashton, by the way," he said.

"I'm Maven, but you can call me Mave," the guy said, smiling. He then raised his eyebrow at me and asked as if he were from the 1900s, "And this young lady? What would her name be?"

I stiffened and cursed myself for not being able to respond. He's just a boy, he won't hurt me....he probably thinks I'm a coward.....he probably thinks I'm ugly and-

"This is Aspen, my sister," Ashton told him while clasping his hand over mine from under the table, easing my nerves. Mave looked at me a little weird for not replying to him but seemed to shake it off as he continued to talk to my brother.

Turns out we have had second period with Mave, too, but this time we made sure to sit next to him instead of in front of him. Even though he and I weren't exactly friends like him and Ashton probably were at this point, the fact that Ash felt comfortable with him made me feel reassured. I was happy he didn't force me to talk to him, and I was especially happy that Ash seemed to really like him.

Since we have Lunch A, it is right after second period, Ash and I followed Mave to the Cafeteria.

"Y'all should sit with me," Mave said as he was approaching a table. Of all guys. There were four other boys sitting there glancing at us. I took a step back as Ash looked at me and without a second to spare, he answered.

"Nah, it's ok. We have to check with our counselor about something, and that'll probably take most of the lunch period," he said while smiling at them, "Thanks for the offer, though."

Once we were out of sight, he squeezed my hand and led me to an empty table on the other side of the cafeteria, the one furthest away from Mave's table.

"I'm sorry," I whispered.

"Excuse me? No. You shouldn't be sorry for anything,"

"No, but you finally made a friend, and we could've just sat with them, and it would've been fine, and you would've had fun, and-"

"Stop it, Aspen. I would never have fun if I knew you were uncomfortable. You come before anyone and anything else. Honestly, I shouldn't have even gotten close to Mave, I'm sorry,"

"No, no! Mave is okay…h-he's nice, I think," I said softly. I looked up to see Ash smiling and nodding.

"Ok, Mave is nice, but we're not ready for his big bulky friends yet," he said, chuckling softly.

"Yea, who knows? They could really hurt your pure soul Ashy," I said, punching him softly. What would I ever do without him by my side? But one thing's for sure, I need to get over this stupid fear.

Since we technically did not have to meet our counselor, the two of us just ate our lunch together, keeping an eye out in case Mave spotted us.

After lunch, we walked to third period, and Mave found us right before we were about to roam around the entire building trying to find our class.

"Heyyy, follow me, my dear friends," he said as he cut between us to go ahead, implying for us to follow him. How he found us? I have no clue. Was I grateful? Hell, yea.

Since the three of us also had third period together, we sat next to each other again. It went smoothly, but I still didn't manage to say a single word to Mave yet, even though I could tell it was bothering him.

It was finally nearing the end of class, and I was putting my books into my backpack when I felt Ash tapping me on the shoulder.

"Do you want me to walk you to your class?" he asked. We didn't have last period together and I tried not to let it get to my head so that I wouldn't have a mental breakdown.

"No it's okay, your class is the completely opposite way and you would be late if you walked me there," I replied, trying to sound confident.

"You think I care? It's fine," he said.

"No, you're not going to be late on the first day. It's okay, I need to learn the way myself anyway," I said, firm in my words. He nodded hesitantly and we walked out of our class. He squeezed my hand as we separated and I was on my way to find this cursed History class of mine. I kept walking with my head down when I realized I was officially lost. Of course I was. I was about to retrace my steps when I felt my head smack into a body. I quickly looked up while rubbing my head and saw that it was one of the boys from Mave's table.

"Watch where you're going, will you," he snarled without taking as much as a glance at me.

"Excuse me? You're the one who bumped into me," I said, slightly ticked off. He looked at me, well down at me because he's about two heads taller than me. And then he took a couple steps closer to me, and as much as I wanted to back away, I hated that he would be able to tell I was scared. Fake it till I make it. I was still not able to look at him, but it took all my strength to not run away.

"Aren't you the little chick who Mave asked to sit with us at lunch? Probably saw us and chickened out, huh?" he said, smirking. I felt my ears burn, because he was right. I did chicken out. I was about to walk away when he grabbed my shoulder and turned me to face him. I stumbled in shock and almost screeched from the feel of his hand around my arm. He looked at me annoyed and pushed me against the wall before smirking and walking away. I winced as I felt my side throb. The stab wound still didn't heal and that shove did more damage than I thought it would.

"Pfft, look at you. Already getting bullied?" I heard a voice say. I looked up to see Ezekiel looking at me. I widened my eyes at his words and backed away, concealing the pain from my wound.

"I mean, it's only inevitable considering how pathetic you are. Did your dear brother also get sick of you? Is that why he left you?" he mocked. I bit my tongue to keep myself from saying anything and lifted my head to show him my defiance. Soon, some other boys trailed beside Ezekiel, and when he saw them, they just started walking away as if I never even existed.

Once I finally found my class, I was already five minutes late and I looked for an empty seat with my head hanging low. I barely even acknowledged the teacher and just put my head on the desk, making sure no one could see my face.

"C'mon, it's only been a couple minutes since I left you alone, did you miss me that much?" I heard that familiar voice say. I lifted my head from my desk to be met with Mave's playful smile. The smile dropped the moment he saw my face.

"What happened?" he asked in confusion. I just turned away and put my head back down. I heard him sigh and felt his eyes burning holes into my head. Please don't say anything, please don't say anything, please don't say anything.

I hope you guys liked this chapter! Please vote and follow!

Love,

Day Lilac ♡

Back Home

Aspen POV

Curse my science teacher, because that woman wants us to go outside of the school, to the forests surrounding it, and look for living beings. And they can't be human. I trudged behind the class as we walked to the forests, everyone having their species-identifying sheets in hand. The first animal I saw was a frog, so I quickly marked it on my paper and explained its characteristics. As I was minding my own business, Cole, who I learned was the self-proclaimed clown and troublemaker of the class, came up to me, seeming to have a hidden agenda. I internally groaned as I turned to face him. Why do I always encounter trouble whenever Ash isn't with me?

"So new girl, where you from?" he asked. I couldn't detect any malice or bad intentions from the question so I honestly didn't know how to answer. Or more specifically, I just didn't know the answer. I stared at him blankly, and I think that ticked him off a little.

"What, you don't know? Are you some foster kid or sum? No parents?" he probed. No parents. Those words affected me more than I thought they would. I do have a....dad....I guess. But does he even consider me to be his daughter? Am I worthy enough to be his daughter? And then I felt Cole give me a slight push. Not to hurt me, but to shake me out of my thoughts. But I don't like any contact at all. So I slapped his hand away and glared at him. That angered him. Because then he muttered a couple of profanities and tried to get closer to me.

"Cole, what are you doing?" Mave said as he walked towards us with his hands tucked in his pockets.

"This girl thinks she's all-that and it's getting on my nerves," Cole responds. When I tried backing away, he pulled me towards him and I brought my hands up to shield my face. Then almost immediately, Mave pulls Cole and shoves him away from me. I felt a sense of relief wash over me as my personal space wasn't invaded anymore and I was able to breathe normally again. I met Mave's eyes which seemed to be asking if I was alright and I subtly nodded while maintaining eye contact. I hope he got the message that I was trying to say thank you as well. He smiled at me softly and walked away.

We ended up dismissing from the forestry area, and since it was the last period, I had to find my way to the parking lot where Sebastian said their car would be.

"If you're taking the bus, you can follow that girl over there," Mave said as he pointed to a girl, whose name I learned to be Ashley.

"But if you're going to the parking lot, you can follow me," he said and started walking. I was glad he didn't phrase anything as a question and didn't expect me to answer. I silently followed him until we were at the parking garage, where I think only students who drove to school were allowed to park. I looked around for the black Mercedes we came in, but instead, my eyes found Ashton.

"Aspen!" he yelled as he ran over to me. I stepped closer and smiled widely, happy to see him. He gave me a quick side hug and focused his attention on Mave curiously.

"Hey man, what's up?" he asked Mave, obviously confused as to why he was here and with me.

"So turns out your sis and I have fourth period together, and I just showed her the way here," Mave responded while scratching the back of his head. Ashton smiled at him and shot me a glance, probably trying to gauge how I felt about that. I just shrugged.

Once Mave left, we went over to the car and saw Sebastian waiting for us. He didn't so much as look at us before getting into the driver's seat. When we got into the car, I realized the twins were already seated. I suddenly felt a little bad for making them wait.

"What took you so long?" Ezekiel asked with a snarl to his tone. Ashton just ignored him so I decided to ignore him too.

"Hey, answer your brother if he asks you a question," Sebastian said from the front with a steady firm tone. So is Sebastian siding with Ezekiel now too?

"We just had some trouble finding the way here," Ashton responded. I looked at him and noticed he was clutching his hands together, probably in frustration. This was just reminding me of how much of a terrible day I was having, and my mood suddenly turned sour.

"Where's your other sister?" Ezekiel asked again. 'your other sister.' As if she wasn't his sister. Right on cue, the car door opened and Tammie's face came into view. She had a small smile but it disappeared once she saw my expression. She quickly looked around the car and saw Ezekiel angrily glaring at her. She ignored him and sat down. I don't know if he was just nicer to her, but Ezekiel didn't question why she came late even though she came later than us. Either way, I was just happy to see her again. Not happy enough to completely eradicate my sour mood though.

"How was your day?" Tamsyn whispered to me.

"It was...ok," I replied back. "How about yours?" I asked. She shrugged and gave me an 'I'll tell you later' look. The rest of the car ride back home was pretty silent.

~ back home ~

The moment we got home, the three of us debriefed on our days. Tamsyn told us about the friends she made and Ashton gushed about Mave. I decided it was best if I didn't mention my unfortunate encounters.

Our conversation was interrupted by a sudden knock on the door. After a couple of seconds, Everett's head popped into the room with a big smile.

"Hey guys, just letting you know that Ezekiel, Sebastian, and I are going out real quick," he said.

"Where are y'all going?" Tamsyn asked.

"Uuh, just family...business stuff," he said hastily before running off. The three of us looked at each other and just shrugged. I guess it wasn't our problem. Family business stuff after all. We decided to finish our homework and just hang out until dinner.

If y'all want more updates, pleaseee vote and comment! It'll be really helpful and give me much more motivation :)

Love,

Day Lilac ♡

Shaken Up

At Dinner

Tamsyn POV

"Ok kids, so your cousin sister will be coming to visit in a couple of weeks alright?" Francesco started to say when we were all seated at the dinner table. Of course, Ash, Aspen, and I didn't have any particular reaction to this piece of news but the other boys seemed to be quite happy. For once, Ezekiel didn't have a scowl on his face and Sebastian looked mildly interested in the conversation. They started asking questions, why was she coming, when was she coming, how long was she staying, and it just went on. With the news of this cousin sister, all the following conversations were about her. I think they forgot it was our first day of school...ever....but that didn't really matter. I don't know why I thought they would actually care to hear about how school went anyways.

I was used to Sebastian and Ezekiel ignoring us, but for some reason, even Theodore and Kyler didn't make any effort to engage or talk to us. Apart from the occasional smiles from Everett, everything else made me feel more like a visitor than part of the family.

It's finally Friday now and the last couple of days at school were pretty good. I became closer to Alina and Rosie, but I was still having a hard time with the boy. Who's name I still don't know.

"Move, will ya," speak of the devil. I grunted as I moved my backpack over so the boy could sit on his seat.

I wasn't feeling my best today because I was drowning myself in questions as to why our other siblings were still giving us the cold shoulder. I thought on Monday it was just because they were busy or preoccupied with work, but it has lasted the entire week now. On top of that, Francesco has been on a business trip since Wednesday for who knows how long, leaving Theodore in charge.

"Tamsyn!" our teacher yelled, startling me. I whipped my head to her as she made her way towards me angrily.

"I've been calling you for the past two minutes, young lady," she said.

"Oh, I'm sorry," I replied. She tsked and shot me a harsh glare before walking back to her desk. I sighed and went back to dwelling in my thoughts.

"Tam, she's coming again," I hear the boy say. Tam? He already has a nickname for me while I don't even know what his name is. I look up just in time to lock eyes with our teacher and give her a quick smile in an attempt to tell her I've been paying attention the entire time. I train my eyes back on the boy to see him roll his eyes at me.

"Would it hurt to pay attention? Because of you, she keeps looking at our table," the boy grunts.

"Says the one that's glued to his phone," I muttered. Usually, after this class, I walk to lunch with the boy since we still sit together in lunch, but today I had to stay a little longer to talk to my teacher and he didn't even consider waiting for me. At this point, it was fine because I knew the way there.

When I got to our usual table, my heart dropped seeing it empty. I looked around and at the lunch line thinking that maybe they were still getting their lunch. After about five minutes of searching for them, I decided to just sit down at the table. I knew they were all at school since they were with me in first period, so I was a little distraught at their absence of them.

As I was sitting there hoping to see them walking towards me, I instead saw someone who looked all too familiar. Levi. Immediately, my eyes widen and my hand reaches to my back pocket where I had a pocket knife stored just for good measure. How the hell did they find us so fast? His eyes landed on mine, and they locked for a good ten seconds before he smirked and walked away.

I could feel the anger rise in me as I debated what to do about this information. Right then I felt a hand on my shoulder, and my instincts got the best of me. I grabbed the hand and pulled it towards me, ready to jab the person in the neck. The same time I realized it was just Rosie, was the moment the boy grabbed my hand and pushed me away from her, making my head hit a pillar that was beside me.

"Hey! What was that for?" The boy asked with malice in his voice as he checked to see if Rosie was okay.

"I-i'm sorry, I thought it was someone else. I'm so sorry Rosie, are you okay?" I asked, hoping she could sense the genuity in my voice. Alina was also checking up on Rosie and before either of them could say anything, the boy came up to me.

"You know what, there was always something weird about you. I thought it was just cuz you're new, but no, you're just sick." he spat at me.

"Sterling! Bro, she said it was just an accident," Alina said immediately. Sterling. So that's what his name is.

"Yeah, I'm okay. She was probably just startled," Rosie said as she got up and smiled at me.

"Sure, an accident," Sterling said as he rolled his eyes. For some reason, his words hurt more than I thought they would. I was under the impression that maybe we were starting to get along, but his words prove that he's just been putting up with me.

Aspen POV

There was something off about today. I don't know what it is, but ever since I got up this morning, I had a bad feeling.

I was sitting in fourth period, minding my own business, when the class door opened to reveal a boy. Usually, I wouldn't pay any attention to things like this, but this was someone I just couldn't ignore. Without even realizing it, I started trembling. Not because I was scared, but because I couldn't stand the mere disgusting presence of him. Levi smirked as he walked past me and sat next to the empty seat right next to Mave, who was directly behind me. Throughout the rest of class, I made it a point to completely ignore and avoid him at any cost. The only thing that made me sick to the stomach was how Levi and Mave were 'getting to know each other'. But could I blame Mave? At one point, even I was playing 'getting to know each other' with Levi.

Usually, I would walk to the parking lot with Mave after class, but I wasn't feeling it today, especially after I heard Mave offer to show Levi the way there. You best believe, that the moment the bell rang, I sprinted outside of that door. As I was lowkey running to the parking lot, trying to make sure Mave didn't catch up to me, I saw Everett walking on the other side of the hallway with his eyes trained on his phone. Without thinking, I ran towards him and stood beside him, letting his body cover mine as I saw Mave and Levi walk past us. I let out a sigh of relief and let myself relax until I was startled by a voice.

"Um, Aspen?" Everett said.

"Oh! Sorry, haha. I forgot the way to the parking lot so when I saw you I just had to make sure I wouldn't lose sight of you," I said.

"Ah okay, for a second it seemed like you were hiding from someone," he said, chuckling a little. But then he paused when he saw my expression and looked at me with concern.

"...who was it? Who were you hiding from?" he said, with a serious tone.

"No no, I swear I wasn't hiding from anyone!" I said to him, trying to play it off cool. But instead his expression got colder, and I didn't understand why. Why would he care if I was hiding from someone? He never even associates with me in school anyway. His eyes narrowed at me and his once playful smile was long gone.

"Aspen, don't lie to me-"

"I'm NOT!"

Without giving me a chance to try to explain myself or the situation, he grabbed my hand and speed walked to the car. I struggled in his grip until we got to the car and then he pushed me inside before getting in after me.

"Did something happen?" Sebastian asked, eyeing me, because apparently only I could do something wrong.

"She's lying about something," Everett responded. Sebastian stayed silent, which I learned was him demanding more information. After Everett supplied him with his information, to which all I could do was roll my eyes, Sebastian stayed silent but I could tell he was also angry at me. Soon enough, the rest of the siblings got to the car and when Tamsyn got it, I noticed she looked a little shaken up. I decided to ask about it when we were alone.

If y'all want more updates, pleaseee vote and comment! It'll be really helpful and give me much more motivation :)

Alsoo, do you guys want to know more about Ash, Aspen, and Tamsyn's past? And do you think the other brothers should find out more about their past soon?

Love,

Day Lilac ♡

Things Like That Don't Fly Here

Aspen POV

When we got to the house, I just had time to use the bathroom before I got called into the office.

"What? Why, does she need to go there?" Ashton asked Kyler when he came to tell me to go to the office.

"We just need to ask about something," Kyler responded. I didn't want Ashton to come with me because I sure as hell didn't want that to be the way he potentially found out that Levi had found us. So I quickly followed Kyler while giving Ash the 'I'm fine' look.

When I got to the office, I was surprised to see ALL of the brothers in there, with Theodore in the middle since Francesco (dad) was still on his business trip. Although I've gotten somewhat used to these men, the sheer number of them against me was quite unsettling. And I still didn't understand why any of this was a big deal. All I frikkin did was go stand next to Everett.

"I heard something happened at school today," Theodore started.

"I just-" I tried saying but was cut off by Ezekiel.

"Did he ask you to speak?" he snapped at me as if whatever I would have to say was so insignificant I should just cut off my tongue. I quickly shook my head and kept it down, waiting for whatever were to come next. I felt a few steps come closer to me and I shuddered while taking a step back.

"Listen, we've been going easy on you because you just lost your mom and we know this is a big change for you, but that does NOT under any circumstance mean you can break one of the rules we set for you," Theodore said. That's when I remembered the few rules that we were told in the beginning and one of the biggest one, which was that we can not tell any lies.

"May I speak now?" I asked cautiously, still keeping my eyes trained on the floor.

"Look at me and speak," Theodore ordered. So I obliged. "Tell me why you were hiding and why you were lying," he said.

"I just...didn't want...uh... someone to see me walking away," I said, sounding unsure to even myself. I looked to Kyler, hoping he would give me a sense of comfort but all I saw was his narrowed eyes trained at me.

"Why? Did someone do something to you?" Kyler asked me.

"N-no! I just didn't want to walk with him,"

"Him?" Everett, Theodore, and Kyler all asked in synch, seemingly getting even more agitated with me. I flinched and backed up a bit more.

"Did 'he' do something? What did he do? Who is he?" Kyler asked all at once. I didn't know what to say. We decided not to tell anyone about anything that happened to us, or about Blake, or The Guild. Keeping that part of us in wraps may make them actually accept us. So I know I can't tell them about Levi, because then I would have to explain why I was hiding from him.

"It was nothing! No one. No one did anything. Could I not have just wanted to stand next to Everett? Was it wrong to feel safe with someone for once!? Is it wrong that for once in my life, I FELT LIKE I HAD SOMEONE WHO WOULDN'T LET ME GET HURT!?!?" I couldn't hold it in anymore.

"I don't care what you think of me, but I'm not going to let you berate me when I didn't do anything wrong!" I snapped and swiftly turned, hoping to just run out of this room. Instead, I was greeted by Ezekiel's deathly glare as he stepped in front of me.

"What the f**k do you think you're doing?" he seethed.

"Ok Ezekiel, language," Kyler chided from behind him, but right now I wasn't focused on him, the only thing that was circling my mind was how much hate I could see in Ezekiel's eyes. They weren't like Levi's eyes, which show lust, pity, and amusement, no, Ezekiel's eyes showed hate and anger. And it was directed at me.

"You think you rule this house? That you can just turn your back on Theo and act like nothing happened? Even I can't do that and expect to go unpunished, much less you. You're nothing in this family, remember that," he sneered at me right before getting pulled from in front of me by Everett. I didn't care at that point. Since I wasn't anything in this family, I took one more glance at Kyler and Theo's disapproving eyes and left the room without a word.

I stormed into Tamsyn's room and banged the door behind me, hoping the other boys would hear it.

"Hey, what happened?" Tamsyn and Ashton both asked me at the same time, worry all over their faces. After I told them what happened, to say they were mad would be an understatement. Of course, they had a different perspective, since they knew who Levi was and that only made them madder. I almost didn't want any of them to go downstairs for dinner because I knew nothing good would come from interacting with them. I already decided I wasn't going to go.

A little while later, we heard the doorbell ring and then a girl's voice through the halls. We put two and two together and figured it was probably that cousin of ours that was supposed to be coming soon.

At around dinner time, Everett came to tell us to come down for dinner. The entire time, he wouldn't even look me in the eye. Probably because, no, definitely because he was the reason everyone in this house hated me even more now.

"We're not coming," Ashton said defiantly. At this, Everett narrowed his eyes and crossed his arms.

"Listen, don't make the situation worse than it already is," he said.

"That's funny, coming from you," Ashton spat back and stepped closer to him. "We're not coming. Deal with it."

I know for a fact that if it were anyone other than Everett who came to call us, they would've practically forced us out of the room, but instead, he just sighed and left.

Tamsyn POV

I was mad. Not just at how they treated my little sister. Not just because we're going to have to deal with Levi soon. Not just because our mom was dead. Not just because we have no family anymore. I was mad at everything.

It was Saturday so I was prepared to deal with the boys when I went downstairs, but what I completely forgot about was the cousin.

"Oh hey look who it is! Is this the kidnapped princess or the bastard twin?"

My eyes widened as I turned to face the blue-eyed brunette standing in front of me with her arms at her hips and a taunting smile on her face.

"Heh. I wouldn't call her a princess. More like a prick on our side that we were relieved from. But then of course unfortunately the pricks always end up coming back" Ezekiel said as he got up from the couch and walked to the brunette.

"Aah, so you're Tamsyn," she said, eyeing me from head to toe. At that point, the rest of the brothers, except Sebastian all walked in to the living room.

"Um, yes," I replied, about to go the kitchen to get myself something to eat, when I was halted by her screechy voice.

"Hey don't turn your back on me like your stupid sissy did."

You best believe, that if it was just us two, I would've had her on the ground, begging to be released by now. But I couldn't do that with everyone watching. I could tell Kyer didn't like that she called Aspen my "stupid sissy," but before he could say anything, she got a phone call and walked away. I shut my eyes and took a deep breath, trying to regain my composure before opening them to glare at…really anything, but it ended up being right at Theodore. And he didn't like that.

"Tamsyn. Don't look at me like that. And you know you guys are in trouble," he said. I looked at him in confusion, because what did I do wrong?

"Dinner last night," Kyler said, after noticing that I didn't know what he was talking about.

"I think we're going to have to go through our rules once more and delve deeper into the consequences," Theo said. "Also tell Aspen that she can't avoid the consequences of her actions. Things like that don't fly here."

Let Them Be Scared

T amsyn POV

I was sitting at the table eating my cereal when the cousin sat next to me.

"Um, by the way, what's your name?" I asked.

"Marila," she replied, seemingly disgusted that I didn't already know. Which made me realize how much I didn't know about this family. Much to my dislike, the rest of the boys came and sat at the table as well. It's like Marila was a magnet, wherever she was the boys went. They chatted with each other for the next like 10 mins while I picked at my cereal, and when I was finally about to get up to leave, Marila called out my name.

"Soo Tamsyn. How has your life been?" I tried not to visibly stiffen as I managed a small smile.

"Good,"

"Yea, I'm sure the death was such a shock," I looked away immediately and trained my eyes on an empty chair as she continued. "And figuring out you have five other brothers must have been mind-blowing," she said.

"I guess..." was all I could muster. From the corner of my eye, I saw Sebastian raise an eyebrow.

" 'I guess' is all you can muster up for your mom dying?" he said coldly. I quickly shook my head and was about to expand on my answer when Ezekiel chuckled.

"Yeah, she's probably been pampered her whole life by her sl**ty mommy and was just happy to come home to a house like this," he said as he laughed with Marila.

"Don't disrespect my mom like that," I whispered.

"What did you say?" Ezekiel mocked.

"I SAID KEEP MY MOTHER OUT OF YOUR FILTHY MOUTH!" I yelled at him. I got up from my chair, and at the same time so did Theodore and Kyler.

"Tams-" Kyler started but I cut him off.

"What? Don't tell me you're just going to stand there and let him badmouth my mother. My mom. The mom that tried her best to protect us even when she was at her weakest," I said.

"Ezekiel, apologize," Theodore said, his body facing Ezekiel. He seemed like he wanted to say something snarky back, but one look from Theodore made him rethink that and he muttered a small 'sorry' to me. But the damage was done. I tried so hard to forget about mom. As bad as it sounds, the more I didn't think about her, the less it hurt. But now, she wasn't here to protect us and to love us. We're on our own. Fighting back tears, I stormed upstairs and joined Ash and Aspen in the 'we're not leaving our room' club.

Theodore POV

I was disappointed. First in Aspen because of what happened yesterday, and then because of Tamsyn. I was disappointed... up until I saw those tears in her beautiful baby blue eyes. The eyes I haven't seen cry in the last thirteen years. The eyes I longed to see for over a decade, and now I'm the reason she's crying. I wanted to wrap her in a hug the moment she ran to her room, but I also knew that she's got to learn some rules. And pampering her is not going to help.

"Ezekiel, don't mention her mom like that," I said firmly. "You know it's probably a sensitive topic. And since when were you allowed to taunt your siblings like that?"

"Kyler, let's go to my office," I told him as I made my way to the office, Kyler right behind me. I was halted right outside of Tamsyn's door when I heard sniffles coming from inside. I immediately looked at Kyler, who's face held a mixture of regret and conflict. As he was about to reach out his hand to knock on the door, but I grabbed it and held it midair as I shook my head.

"They need to learn," I told him. And although I knew it was killing him inside, I led him to my office, leaving the sniffling behind us.

"We need to put some consequences in place for them. It obviously can't be the same as the ones Seb, Ezekiel, and Everett have. They've been raised in the mafia, the others haven't. For all we know, Ezekiel is right. They are weak," I said after Kyler closed the door.

"Don't talk like we can blame that on them. They were taken from us and were raised by that snake. Who knows how they've been raised," he replied.

"I know we can't blame them. If anything we're the ones in the wrong for taking so long to find them. But now, it's our job to make sure they know how to behave and stay safe," I said.

"What should we do? Ground them? Spank them? Can we even do that to the girls?" he asked.

"We also can't have double standards. And....that is the mafia way. Whether they're girls or not. They're part of this family," I said, heavily sighing.

Tamsyn's POV

I decided not to think about what happened and face-timed Alina and Rosie instead. It was unlike me to do something like that, but those two are always asking me to FaceTime, and I'm always declining it. So this time, I decided to actually call them. They both pick up on the second ring and look as astonished as I do that I even mustered up the courage to call them.

"Tammie!?" they both exclaimed at the same time.

"Did something happen? Are you okay?" Immediately followed, which startled me because how did they know?

"Um...no everything's fine," I answered meekly.

"Girl, c'mon. I know we haven't known each other for a long time, but if there's one thing that I do know - it's that you NEVER call us," Alina said, smiling slightly but still having a concerned expression.

"Yeah, you know you can tell us anything right?" Rosie added.

"Yea...but right now I kind of just want to take my mind off some things," I answered sincerely. They both smiled in understanding and (figuratively) took me to another world. A world where I forgot about this messed-up family.

Theodore POV

"Sebastion, call Ashton, Aspen, and Tamsyn for dinner. Don't take no for an answer," I said.

While Seb went to get them, I decided to have a little chat with Ezekiel.

"Listen, I know you're pissed. But that doesn't mean you can have an attitude. Don't take out your anger of mom on to them. I'm warning you, just don't even try with the snarky comments today," I said, as I held eye contact with him.

"Yeah bro, they're probably scared shit of you," Everett added as he put his arm around his twin brother.

"Let them be scared. It's not like I want to be friends with them," Ezekiel commented. I gave him a stern glare and he shut up.

Is That What They Think Of Us?

A spen POV

When we came down for dinner, everyone was seated at the dinner table - including Marila. I made it a point to avoid eye contact with everyone as I sat down. There was a thick air of silent tension until Marila spoke up.

"So Ashton, you're the only one I haven't seen so far," she said. All eyes turned to Ashton, and that's when I remembered that no one had seen him in a while other than Tammie and I.

"You're quite timid for a Fontana man, aren't you?" she continued, eyeing Ashton. As always, he just ignored her.

"Heh, well you're definitely just as disrespectful as your sister," she said as she side eyed Tamsyn and I. I grabbed both Ash and Tamsyn's hands from under the table, willing them not to make a big deal out of it. We're already in trouble and there's no point in making it worse.

"Oh? What happened, y'all are awfully quiet now?" she asked.

"They must have learned their lesson," Theodore said firmly. I wanted to roll my eyes at the, but I controlled myself. The rest of that dinner was painstaking and pure torture. Marila and the other boys (except Ash) were talking about a bunch of random stuff while we tried our best to finish our food fast. As soon as we were done eating, we asked to be excused and Theodore let us go.

Third POV

"Why did you guys even let them come back?" Marila asked right when the other three left the table.

"I would ask the same thing," Ezekiel retorted.

"They're our family, our siblings. Why wouldn't we bring them back?" Kyler said.

"Well, yeah...but they were raised by her. Who knows what type of people they are," Marila said with a disgusted tone.

"I agree, they haven't told us much about their past lives. And we shouldn't just let random people come into our family like that, especially with what we do," Sebastian spoke up.

"You should have just let them go to a foster family or something," Marila snarked as she grabbed a drink. "It would've saved you from all this trouble. And plus now you have to protect them too."

"Psh yea, and Theo, did dad even do a blood test to make sure those twins are even his? Didn't that woman run away with some man?" Ezekiel said with a matter-of-fact tone. This question even got Theodore to look at him as if he was thinking about it for the first time. He looked doubtful, almost.

"Ezekiel that's taking it too far. Ashton and Aspen are our siblings!" Everett interjected quickly.

"Sure, they're definitely her children, but can we really call that being our full siblings?" Ezekiel said. Suddenly, Theodore got up from his chair, resulting in everyone following suit. Kyler put a hand on Theo's shoulder as if to calm him down.

"Don't tell me you're actually considering that..." Kyler asked hesitantly.

Tamsyn POV

Let's be real, we were barely out of the dining room when Marila started speaking, and as it concerned us, it was only natural that we listen in. Do I regret it? Not really. Am I angry at what they said? Hell yea. But before I could explode and tell them that Ash and Aspen were their full siblings and that our mom would never cheat, Ashton tugged on my hand urgently.

'Let's go,' he mouthed. I obliged since it seemed like Theodore might walk this way. We tiptoed up the stairs as if we were ghosts, and kudos to all of our training in The Guild because it paid off.

Once we got into our room, I looked the twins in the eye and tried to make out what was going through their brains.

"I'm surprised it took them so long to have that thought," Ash said as he sat on the bed.

"Yeah, I'm surprised making us have a blood test wasn't the first thing they did," Aspen added. And as much as I agreed with them, I could hear the pain and sadness in their voices.

"I miss mom," Aspen whispered as she lay her head on the pillow.

"Do you think...they'll let us visit her grave?" Ashton asked me.

"Um...I mean I don't know why they wouldn't. We could ask," I replied. Our conversation was interrupted by a knock on the door and Theodore's face after he opened it.

"Be ready tomorrow morning. We're going to the hospital," and then he left, barely letting us even process what he said.

Ashton POV

The next morning, we got ready and met the others downstairs. It was just Theodore, Kyler, and Sebastian going with us, and I already knew the experience was going to be much better than if Ezekiel was going to come with us. By the end of the day, he would probably make us wish we really weren't his full biological siblings. No one technically told us why we were going to the hospital, and I guess they were never planning to.

For some reason, they made us go so early in the morning, it was 7 AM, so the entire car ride to the hospital was personally spent in dreamland.

Theodore POV

Looking at the twins from the rearview mirror, I wondered again if taking this DNA test was necessary. But then I reminded myself that with that woman, anything was possible.

When we got to the hospital, I woke the twins up and noticed they were both in a very grumpy mood. Even more grumpier than usual. I smiled slightly at the similarity between them and Everett and Ezekiel. Whenever they're woken up after a long car ride, they're the grumpiest people ever.

I led them to our family doctor's office and let the twins sit inside the examination room, while the rest of us were outside. Tamsyn insisted on staying with them, but the doctor advised her not to and she couldn't argue against it. Before they took the blood samples, I was talking with the doctor outside of the examination room door about what he was about to do.

Full-siblings or not, those twins were my responsibility and family, so I needed to make sure everything was perfect. After I was done talking to him, he went to get some supplies while I waited outside the door. Soon after, Sebastian came up and stood next to me.

"Where's everyone else?" I asked him.

"They're in the waiting room. Tamsyn's sweating her head off, though. It's almost like she's the one who's about to get their blood drawn or something," Sebastian said, shaking his head slightly.

"They've really got a special relationship don't they?" I replied. "I wonder if we'll ever be able to get that relationship back, at least with Tamsyn," I said, reminiscing about the blissful time before the terrible incident happened.

Sebastian and I both turned to the door when we heard voices start speaking.

"So, let's say this dna test comes back negative...what do you think they're going to do?" we heard Ashton say. Sebastian immediately looked at me with scrunched eyes.

"How do they know we're here for a dna test?" he asked me in a hushed tone.

"I don't know, I didn't tell them. Unless one of the other boys told them ...they shouldn't know," I responded.

"Pfft, probably throw us out in the streets or something," we then heard Aspen say. My hands immediately fisted up at the fact that she could even think that we would do something like that.

"You really think so?" Ashton asked.

"Bruh, they already hate me. They don't give a damn about what happens to us, believe me," Aspen said.

"You think they'd...like kill us or something?" Ashton asked, which was met with silence from Aspen.

I looked at Sebastian and saw the hurt and confusion swirl through his eyes. I grabbed his arm and walked a bit further away from the door, so they wouldn't hear us.

"Is that what they think of us?" Sebastian asked me, staring into my eyes.